Instant Parallel Processing with Gearman

Learn how to use Gearman to build scalable distributed applications

John Ewart

PUBLISHING

BIRMINGHAM - MUMBAI

Instant Parallel Processing with Gearman

First published: July 2013

Production Reference: 1230713

Published by Packt Publishing Ltd.
Livery Place
35 Livery Street
Birmingham B3 2PB, UK.

ISBN 978-1-78328-407-8

www.packtpub.com

Credits

Author

John Ewart

Reviewer

Josh Black

Acquisition Editor

Vinay Argekar

Commissioning Editor

Priyanka Shah

Technical Editor

Mausam Kothari

Project Coordinator

Michelle Quadros

Proofreader

Bernadette Watkins

Graphics

Ronak Dhruv

Production Coordinator

Prachali Bhiwandkar

Cover Work

Prachali Bhiwandkar

Cover Image

Prachali Bhiwandkar

About the Author

John Ewart is a systems architect, software developer, and lecturer. He has designed and taught courses at a variety of institutions including the University of California, California State University and local community colleges covering a wide range of computer science topics including Java, data structures and algorithms, operating systems fundamentals, UNIX and Linux systems administration, and web application development. In addition to working and teaching, he maintains and contributes to a number of open source projects. He currently resides in Redmond, Washington with his wife, Mary, and their two children.

About the Reviewer

Josh Black has been working with computers professionally for 20 years. He has a broad range of experience and expertise including systems and network administration, mobile app development, and production web applications. Josh earned a BS in computer science with a minor in math from California State University, Chico, in 2005. He currently resides in Chico, California, with his wife Rachel, and their four children.

www.packtpub.com

Support files, eBooks, discount offers and more

You might want to visit www.packtpub.com for support files and downloads related to your book.

Did you know that Packt offers eBook versions of every book published, with PDF and ePub files available? You can upgrade to the eBook version at www.packtpub.com and as a print book customer, you are entitled to a discount on the eBook copy. Get in touch with us at service@packtpub.com for more details.

At www.packtpub.com, you can also read a collection of free technical articles, sign up for a range of free newsletters and receive exclusive discounts and offers on Packt books and eBooks.

packtlib.packtpub.com

Do you need instant solutions to your IT questions? PacktLib is Packt's online digital book library. Here, you can access, read and search across Packt's entire library of books.

Why Subscribe?

- ✦ Fully searchable across every book published by Packt
- ✦ Copy and paste, print and bookmark content
- ✦ On demand and accessible via web browser

Free Access for Packt account holders

If you have an account with Packt at www.packtpub.com, you can use this to access PacktLib today and view nine entirely free books. Simply use your login credentials for immediate access.

Table of Contents

Instant Parallel Processing with Gearman

Welcome to the *Instant Parallel Processing with Gearman*. This book has been written to show you all you need to know to get started using Gearman. You will learn the history of Gearman, how to run your own servers, write some scripts to process data, and learn some of the more advanced features of Gearman.

This book contains the following sections:

So, what is Gearman? finds out what Gearman is, why it exists, and what you can do with it.

Quick start – building your first components shows you how to set up your own server and interacts with it with some quick examples in Ruby. This section of the book will cover the core concepts of Gearman to get you on your way as quickly as possible to processing jobs using Gearman.

Top 5 features you need to know about helps you learn how to use Gearman beyond simple job submissions. By the end of this section, you will be able to use Gearman and MapReduce methodologies to process large amounts of data, build a pipeline of complex loosely coupled processes that work together to process data using different languages and libraries, offload long-running and complex data analysis and provide real-time feedback to a frontend application, and utilize job coalescing to distribute results to multiple clients while processing the data only one time.

People and places you should get to know tells us that Gearman, like many other open source projects, has a wealth of online resources available. This section will get you started with a number of links to these resources including code examples, libraries, server implementations, mailing lists, and more.

So, what is Gearman?

Gearman is a network-based job-queuing system that was initially developed by Danga Interactive in order to process large volumes of jobs. Its primary design goals were low-latency remote function execution, being able to run code remotely and in parallel, load balancing of job distribution, and supporting writing components in multiple languages.

Although originally written in Perl it is comprised of, at its core, a network protocol that is designed to allow the various components to communicate the lifecycle of a unit of work. Because of this design, there are both servers and client libraries written in multiple languages including Ruby, Perl, PHP, Python, C, C++, and Java.

What this translates into is the ability to design and develop the various components of your architecture in whatever language makes the most sense and have those components communicate easily with one another.

Gearman goes one step further than simply defining a message bus; it formalizes its architecture to focus on units of work. This means that everything in a system using Gearman operates in terms of submitting or working on jobs. To follow this paradigm, Gearman has three main actors: clients who request that work be completed by somebody, the managers (servers) that are responsible for accepting jobs from clients, and then handing those jobs out to workers that ultimately complete the tasks.

Distinguishing features of Gearman

At its core, Gearman is a network protocol; this means that it is not restricted to being used in any one programming language. In fact, there are clients for nearly every (if not every) modern programming language including Java, C#, Python, Perl, Ruby, C, C++, and PHP. If a library does not exist for your language of choice, the protocol is simple enough to rapidly implement at least the basic components required to submit and process jobs. The protocol is well documented and has a very clear request and response cycle.

One of the less obvious benefits of this is that your client can be written in a completely separate language from your worker. For example, a PHP-based web application can submit a request for a job to be processed that is handled by a highly optimized worker written in C for that specific type of task. This allows you to take advantage of the strengths of different languages, and prevents you from being locked into one language or another when building components of your system.

Overview of components

As mentioned before, processing jobs with Gearman requires three different actors:

+ Servers to receive and store jobs in a queue (also known as a manager)
+ Clients that submit jobs to the manager
+ Workers that process these jobs

These components do not need to be on separate machines, though as your system grows you will likely need to dedicate resources to these components to accommodate the growth. Initially, we will run everything on one system because it is the simplest, but we will discuss some options for architecture later on to grow your system from simple to complex.

The conversation between the actors

A very simple view of the communication between the components of an application that uses Gearman looks something similar to the following diagram:

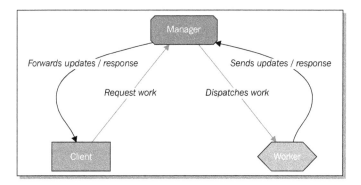

At no point do the worker and the client exchange messages directly; the architecture is designed so that the manager is the middleman and the authoritative source for storing and dispatching jobs.

Behind the scenes, the manager is responsible for storing the jobs in its internal queue. Which, depending on the server and the way it is configured, may or may not be backed by some persistent storage mechanism on disk, in case the server crashes (we will discuss this later on in the book). An example conversation might be as follows:

Client to Manager: I need someone to resize an image; here is the image file I need resized.

Manager to Client: OK, I can do that, I've written down your request.

Manager to Workers who have said they can resize images: Wake up! Someone needs some work done.

Worker to manager: I can do it, give me the next available job!

Manager to worker: Here you go, here is the job and the image to resize.

Worker to manager: All done! Here's the resized image data.

Manager to client: Here you go, your image is resized, here is the resized image.

It is important to note here that the image or some derivative thereof is transferred a total of four times: once from the client to the manager, once from the manager to the worker, and then the resulting resized image is passed back from the worker to the manager, and then from the manager to the client. You may have already noticed that this can quickly become a bottleneck (imagine passing a 1 GB image and a 200 MB resized image back and forth, you've now had to shuffle 2.4 GB of data around).

On top of the data being transferred, the manager may hold this data in memory while it waits for a worker to accept and complete the job. This would mean that you could only queue up a few of these jobs at once without causing the server that is running the manager to start swapping to disk and either significantly degrading performance or running out of memory completely. As you build your systems, try to keep the data that is being passed back and forth as small as possible. One solution to this particular scenario would be to write the image data to a shared data store such as an NFS share or an S3 bucket and pass a path or URL between the client and worker rather than a complete image file.

Usecase – image processing

Image processing is a CPU and IO-bound process. Images need to be loaded from disk into memory and then processed. This often cannot happen in real-time or within the bounds of a normal HTTP request-response cycle. Additionally, some image processing software can benefit from specialized server instances that have access to GPUs for higher throughput image processing. However, these instances can be very cost prohibitive for running as a general-purpose web server. By using Gearman we cannot only achieve a greater level of parallelism, thereby aiding with horizontal scaling, but also be able to use specialized systems to their greatest advantage and optimize the use of resources.

In this case, imagine a web application that provides a web-based photo gallery that needs to accept and resize numerous images from clients. If each image takes 30 seconds to resize, even if the web server were capable of processing 50 requests simultaneously at that rate by performing inline resizing, then the application would only be able to serve just short of two requests per second. In order to be usable, the application must be able to accept and process images as quickly as possible.

In a more advanced architecture, the web server could accept an image from the client, persist the image to a shared data store, and then submit an asynchronous request to the job manager to have the image resized by an available worker. By offloading the image processing as a background task, the web application can respond to client requests much more quickly, thereby allowing the client to store more images while the previously uploaded images are being processed in parallel.

The full sequence diagram for uploading an image using this type of system would resemble the following:

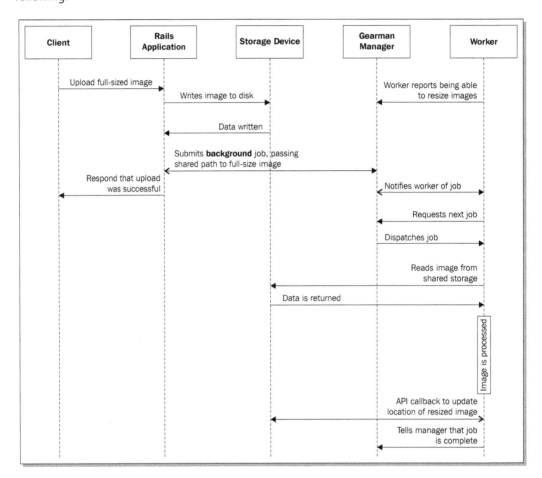

You will notice that the conversation between the end user's client (a web browser in this case) and the web server is very brief, much shorter than it would be if the image processing were to happen in-line with the client's request. For web developers, learning to leverage this type of solution can help to make their application much more responsive by offloading anything that may require significant time, and does not need to be completed synchronously, to the background such as post-sign up API calls, data analysis, image processing, web crawling, and so on are examples of processes that could be performed asynchronously.

Though this usecase examines using Gearman from the context of a web application, it is by no means restricted to being used only by web applications. There are many situations where an application could benefit from using Gearman. Those situations include systems that:

- ✦ Have deadlines within which they have to deliver a response to the user or suffer from a lack of usability. Examples of this are web applications and mobile applications.

- ✦ Operate with limited resources, such as cloud servers, mobile devices, or other systems that may have limited storage or processing power.

- ✦ Work on vast amounts of data and require the ability to process data in parallel, such as geospatial data, large quantities of log or transaction data, and so on.

- ✦ Require, for security purposes, that business logic or other sensitive data and software is to be kept on different servers or networks and so the customer-facing systems cannot complete the request fully by themselves.

- ✦ Process large quantities of small jobs, possibly upwards of millions of jobs per day.

- ✦ Are written using a variety of languages, each suited to a particular task, to solve the problem as a whole and needs a way to pass data between the various components.

Throughout this book we will look at how you can leverage Gearman as a critical part of your infrastructure to build services that are more flexible and can scale horizontally as the demand on the system increases.

Quick Start – building your first components

One of the fastest ways to understand any new technology is to get your hands dirty quickly. To get started, you will have to download and run a Java-based Gearman server, download a Ruby library, and then program two components: a very simple client to submit a request to reverse a string of text, and a worker to perform the reversal.

Step 1 – running a server

There are multiple implementations of the Gearman service. For the exercises in this book, we will use a Java-based Gearman server that is developed and maintained by the author of this book. It has the benefits of being a single file download, running on any platform that supports Java, and having a built-in web-based status dashboard. To download it, you can find it at `http://code.johnewart.net/maven/org/gearman/gearman-server/0.6.0/gearman-server-0.6.0.jar`.

If you haven't already, you will need to install Java for your platform in order to run the daemon. Once you have Java installed, you can execute the JAR for the server by one of a few different methods:

✦ In operating systems that have executable JAR support integrated with the file browser, you can double-click on the JAR file. This will run the server with its default settings.

✦ From a command line (UNIX shell, Windows console) navigate to the directory where you downloaded the JAR file and run the `java -jar gearman-server-0.6.0.jar` command.

Once you have your server running you can test that the things are up and running by connecting to the web management interface through your browser by visiting `http://localhost:8080`. You will see an interface similar to the following screenshot:

From this screen, you can see some basic server statistics such as how many jobs are pending, how many have been processed, how many have been queued, the number of active workers, how long the server has been running, and how much memory the server is using. This is very useful for seeing the overall health of the server, as well as getting a feeling for whether or not you need more workers.

This web management interface is a specific enhancement that the Java Gearman server has—the de-facto C++ manager does not have this available.

Step 2 – downloading a client library

This example involves using the Ruby client library. If you do not have access to a Ruby interpreter, there are many ways to get access to them including setting up a free micro AWS cloud server instance. If you are not comfortable with Ruby, links to libraries and examples in other languages can be found at the end of this book in the section entitled *People and places you should get to know*. However, the examples have comments and are simple enough to demonstrate the workflow, so you should be able to see how things work regardless of your preferred language.

Your first client

The Ruby library is very easy to download and install using RubyGems; it can be installed simply by running `gem install gearman-ruby` from a shell (you may need to be root depending upon how you have Ruby installed).

This exercise helps you to build a very simple client. The client is responsible for creating the jobs in the job queue and has two basic modes of operation, that is, synchronous or asynchronous. In synchronous mode, the client submits the job to the manager and waits for the job to be picked up, worked on, and completed interactively. The client does not disconnect from the server and remains connected throughout the life span of the job. This mode is useful for jobs where the results of the job are needed by the client itself.

The alternative mode of execution is for a job to be executed asynchronously or in the background. In this mode, the client effectively operates in a "fire and forget" mode where the job is submitted to the manager and there is an implicit contract that the job will be completed at some point in the future. These types of jobs tend to be longer-running tasks that would block the client for a long time; by using this mode, the client is free to do other things such as submit more jobs, or perform other tasks.

Writing the client

In the following examples, we will construct a client that requests that a worker pick up a job from the `reverse_string` job queue and waits one day for the job to complete:

```ruby
#!/usr/bin/env ruby

require 'rubygems'

require 'gearman'


# Create a client that connects to the local manager

client = Gearman::Client.new('127.0.0.1:4730')

# Create a set of tasks that the client processes (this is unique to #
the Ruby client, and required for us to wait for them to complete)

taskset = Gearman::TaskSet.new(client)

# Create an actual task for the 'reverse_string' queue with
```

```
# 'reverse this string' as the data to be processed by the worker
task = Gearman::Task.new("reverse_string", "reverse this string")
# In the Ruby client, tasks have an 'on_complete' callback that
# lets you execute some code with the result of a job
task.on_complete {|d| puts d }
# Add the task to the set of tasks to process (this is what
# submits the job)
puts "Submitting job..."
taskset.add_task(task)
# Wait 86,400 seconds for a response (all day)
puts "Waiting for a response..."
taskset.wait(86400)
```

Running your newly created client

Running the Ruby client you have just created is quite simple, you can run it with the following command:

```
[user@host]% ruby client.rb
Submitting job...
Waiting for a response...
```

This example, when run, will wait for an entire day for a result from the manager. The shell will be blocked until the worker in the next section completes the task it is assigned, giving you plenty of time to complete the next step.

Verifying that it was submitted

There are two ways to verify that the job was successfully submitted to the job manager: using the telnet interface or using the web interface. The telnet interface is a text-based commands interface that most, if not all, Gearman servers implement. To interact with it, you may connect to the control port your server is listening on (4730 by default) using any telnet client and issuing the STATUS command followed by a newline or return key. The session should look something like the following:

```
[user@host]% telnet localhost 4730
Trying ::1...
Connected to localhost.
Escape character is '^]'.
status
FUNCTION       TOTAL  RUNNING AVAILABLE_WORKERS
reverse_string 1  0         0
```

If you are using the Java service as just outlined, you can view the web interface and click on the **Queues** link at the top of the page. You will see that a job has been added to the `reverse_string` queue:

	Dashboard	Queues				
	Job Queue		**Workers**	**Size**		**Action**
reverse_string			0	1		Show

Here we can see that there is only one job queue that the manager knows about and that it is named `reverse_string`, it has zero workers, and it has a queue size of one. This is the job we just created using our client. As you can see, queues are created on-demand; there is no need to configure the daemon with a list of queues that exist. Once a job queue is created, it will persist until the service stops running, even when it has no more jobs that are waiting.

Step 3 – our first worker

Workers provide the mechanism for completing units of work in the system. Our first example will register itself as being able to process jobs in the queue `reverse_string` and then accept jobs from that queue, reversing the data, and returning the results:

```ruby
require 'rubygems'
require 'gearman'


servers = ['localhost:4730']


# Connect to our list of servers (only one for now)
w = Gearman::Worker.new(servers)


# The Worker class has a method, add_abilitywhich takes
# two arguments, the queue to register and a block that
# is the code to execute for each job taken
w.add_ability('reverse_string') do |data, job|
    puts "Got work!"
    # Dump out what we got
    puts "Job: #{job.inspect} Data: #{data.inspect}"
    # Reverse the data portion
```

```
result = data.reverse
puts "Reverse: #{result} "
# The return value of the block is what gets sent back
# to the manager as the response data for this job
result
```

```
end
```

```
# Execute only one unit of work
w.work
```

Running your newly created worker

Running the Ruby worker is just as simple as running the client. In another terminal, store the preceding example in a file called `worker.rb` and then run it as follows:

```
[user@host]% ruby worker.rb
Got work!
Job: #<Gearman::Worker::Job:0x0000010112f820 @socket=#<TCPSocket:fd 5>,
@handle="e518b247-e7a5-4470-a9ff-0940356dab51"> Data: "reverse this
string"
Reverse: gnirts siht esrever
```

You will notice that now the client has become unblocked and the result that the worker computed (the reverse of the string) will be displayed on the terminal that the client was running in, as follows:

```
[user@host]% ruby client.rb
Submitting job...
Waiting for a response...
gnirts siht esrever
```

Notice that the result generated by the worker is passed from the worker to the manager and then passed back to the client that was waiting for the response. The response is then passed to the `on_complete` block defined in the `client.rb` script and then printed to the console. Each client is going to be a little different, but the typical methods for processing the results of a job are to either block the client until a response comes back or to provide some sort of future callback for the response data.

Step 4 – varying priorities

Gearman jobs have three different priority levels: high, normal, and low. Jobs are removed from a specific queue in that order when a worker polls for work. For example, if you have many jobs in a queue with normal priority and one worker, that worker will continue to pull jobs from the normal-priority queue. If, during the consumption of the queue, a client requests a job be completed with high priority, that job will be the next job to be dispatched to the worker before the remaining normal priority jobs. This allows for work that is more time sensitive (perhaps something a user is waiting on) to be processed before other tasks. Similarly, if you have something that does not need to be processed immediately, it can be placed into the low-priority queue and it will be handled whenever the normal-priority queue is depleted.

In Ruby, these jobs are built by passing an options hash to the `Task` constructor:

```
task = Gearman::Task.new("resize_image", "s3://bucket/image.png",
                         {:priority => "high"})

taskset.add_task(task)
```

In the PECL PHP library, there are separate methods for submitting jobs to the different priority queues:

```
$task = $client->addTaskHigh("reverse", "ratstar", null, "2");
```

Both of the previous code snippets have similar effects; both of them submit a job to the high-priority queue to be processed before normal-priority jobs.

Step 5 – background tasks

Apart from submitting to a different priority queue, jobs can be run in the background. The only significant difference between this and foreground processing is that the client will not block on processing the data, it will fire and forget under the presumption that it will be processed at some point in the future. This is useful for any work that is non-interactive, takes sufficiently long that the client either cannot wait or it is undesirable to wait, will be in a very large queue and may take a very long time to be processed. This means that we will need an alternative method to communicate progress to the client.

In these cases, the client needs to identify that it is submitting a job to be run in the background. The exact mechanism for this will vary with the library that you are using, but they should all support this function in one way or another. For example, submitting tasks in the background using the Ruby library would be done as follows:

```
require 'rubygems'
require 'gearman'

servers = ['localhost:4730']
```

```
# Connect our client
client = Gearman::Client.new(servers)

# Generate a task with the background property being set
task = Gearman::Task.new({'background_job', 'data',
:background => true })

# Submit a job via the client
client.do_task(task)
```

By submitting a background job, the client becomes disconnected from the job. It does not wait for the result, and the manager will not terminate the job if the client disconnects from the manager before the work is completed. Once the manager tells the client that it is accepted, the client does not need to worry about the job any longer.

As is explained later in this book, job managers run by default with their queues in-memory only. As a result, if a manager terminates, it will lose its jobs. Most Gearman servers support persisting job queues to disk for just this reason. See the section on persistence to learn more.

And that's it

Now that we know how to leverage the core features of Gearman, it's time to move on to some more advanced topics including building horizontally scalable systems, using Gearman to perform MapReduce operations, and building systems that do not have single points of failure, allowing us to handle failure of system components.

Top 5 features you need to know about

Gearman is not only a way to process jobs but also a way to build powerful distributed job processing to help horizontally scale your application. We will discuss how to use Gearman to solve a variety of problems such as using the MapReduce methodology to process large amounts of data, build a pipeline of complex loosely coupled processes that work together to process data using different languages and libraries, and offload long-running and complex data analysis and provide real-time feedback to a frontend web application. This section will be a hands-on exploration of how you can leverage both synchronous and asynchronous workers to expand the capability and capacity of your applications, as well as introduce you to the concept of persistent queues, why you might consider using them, and how they will affect your application.

Job handling

In order to understand some of the concepts in this section, you need to know about the lifecycle of a task inside Gearman. Clients submit a request for work by submitting a variation of the SUBMIT_JOB message (the variations have priority and whether or not it's a background job). The manager sends the client a JOB_CREATED message to acknowledge that the job has been received and stored by the manager.

As part of the process of enqueuing a job, the manager is responsible for generating what is known as a **job handle**. A job handle identifies a job in the system and is unique to a given job manager. Typically the job handles are in the format of H:server_name:incremental_number; this way a worker or anyone else interacting with that job knows where the job originated from. However, this format is not mandated and should not be relied upon as not all job managers format job handles in this way. After queuing the job, the manager sends the client a JOB_CREATED message containing the job handle that represents the job inside the manager. Once the manager has accepted the job, the job handle becomes the key used to identify the job. For example, if a client submits a background job, it might need that job handle in order to periodically check the status of that job. When work is completed, an error occurs, or another status related to the job needs to be communicated, the client again uses that job handle to associate the WORK_COMPLETE, WORK_EXCEPTION, WORK_DATA, and so on, messages with the correct job. Once work is completed, it is removed from the work queue and it is important to note that completed is not a synonym for successful.

Completed versus successful

One of the nuances of message-queuing or job-queuing systems is understanding the lifecycle of an entity in the system. In Gearman, there is a best-effort contract between the manager and the client that the work will be completed, where complete may mean that the outcome was successful, generated an error, or failed outright. If a worker disconnects from the manager in the middle of processing a job, then the expected behavior is that the manager will simply requeue the job for another worker to pick up later. In a non-persistent queue, the manager will store jobs only for as long as it is required to deliver the job, or until it terminates. If you need jobs to persist after a manager terminates then you will want to read the section on persistence engines later on in the book.

Unique identifiers and coalescing

Each job has a unique identifier associated with it (in addition to the job handle). The client can set a job's unique identifier. If it is not provided then it will be generated by the manager. When the manager sees multiple jobs with the same unique identifier, it will effectively treat them all as only one job. This allows for the manager to reduce the overall workload by coalescing these job requests into a single unit of work, allowing one worker to handle potentially thousands of client requests by processing a single job. When the manager receives the response from the worker, it will forward that data to all clients requesting jobs with the same unique identifier.

To do this, we will perform the following steps:

1. Write a client that will submit a single job to a job queue with a common unique identifier.
2. Write a worker that will process jobs in that job queue.
3. Run multiple copies of the worker, where each will submit the same job to the manager.
4. Watch the manager coalesce the jobs by processing one job and returning the results to all the clients.

The client

The following client submits a job with a unique identifier set (in this case, it is set to `unique_key`) which the manager uses to identify jobs that are identical. Some libraries will automatically generate a unique identifier that is based on the data that is being submitted so that jobs with the same data will automatically be coalesced for you:

```ruby
#!/bin/env ruby
require 'rubygems'
require 'gearman'
require 'json'
```

```ruby
client = Gearman::Client.new('localhost:4730')
taskset = Gearman::TaskSet.new(client)


taskdata = { :work_data => "work data" }
task = Gearman::Task.new("coalesce", JSON.dump(taskdata),
                         :uniq => "unique_key ")
task.on_complete do |d|
  puts "#{Time.now} Received #{d}"
end


taskset.add_task(task)
puts "#{Time.now} submitted job -- waiting for results."


taskset.wait(100)
```

The worker

The following worker will grab a job from the queue and then sleep for 10 seconds. This gives us enough time to run a few copies of the client to demonstrate that the worker will only get one instance of the job and all the clients will receive the response simultaneously:

```ruby
require 'rubygems'
require 'gearman'
require 'json'


@servers = ['localhost:4730']


puts "Waiting for work..."
w = Gearman::Worker.new(@servers)
w.add_ability('coalesce') do |json_data,job|
  start_time = Time.now
  puts "#{start_time} Received: #{json_data} and sleeping for 10s"
  sleep 10
  "OK -- #{start_time}"
end


loop { w.work }
```

Making it work

To demonstrate this, save the worker code into a file, `worker_coalesce.rb`, and then open a terminal and execute it:

```
[user@host]% ruby worker_coalesce.rb

Waiting for work...
```

The worker will wait for jobs to be submitted by the clients. Next, save the client's code into a file, `client_coalesce.rb`, and open three different terminals. Navigate each of these terminals to where you saved the client, and run one copy of the client in each terminal:

Client 1:

```
[user@host]% ruby client_coalesce.rb

2013-06-27 20:50:15 -0700 submitted job -- waiting for results.
```

Client 2:

```
[user@host]% ruby client_coalesce.rb

2013-06-27 20:50:16 -0700 submitted job -- waiting for results.
```

Client 3:

```
[user@host]% ruby client_coalesce.rb

2013-06-27 20:50:20 -0700 submitted job -- waiting for results.
```

Here we have run three copies of the client, each submitting the same job at three different times: 15, 16, and 20 seconds past the minute. Looking at the worker's output, however, we see that the worker has only received a single job (as expected) immediately after the first client submitted its job:

```
[user@host]% ruby worker_coalesce.rb

Waiting for work...

2013-06-27 20:50:15 -0700 Received: {"work_data":"work data"} and
    sleeping for 10s
```

After the worker sleeps for ten seconds, it will push the results back to the manager who will in turn pass the results along to any clients who are waiting for that job (here all three are waiting for the same job). If you look at the terminals for the clients, you will see that all three of them received the same work data at the same time:

```
[user@host]% ruby client_coalesce.rb

2013-06-27 20:50:15 -0700 submitted job -- waiting for results.

2013-06-27 20:50:25 -0700 Received OK -- 2013-06-27 20:50:15 -0700
```

```
[user@host]% ruby client_coalesce.rb
2013-06-27 20:50:16 -0700 submitted job -- waiting for results.
2013-06-27 20:50:25 -0700 Received OK -- 2013-06-27 20:50:15 -0700


[user@host]% ruby client_coalesce.rb
2013-06-27 20:50:20 -0700 submitted job -- waiting for results.
2013-06-27 20:50:25 -0700 Received OK -- 2013-06-27 20:50:15 -0700
```

Notice that all three clients received the response from the worker to the initial request from the first client. This is because it was the first one in the queue, and so it was pushed out to the worker immediately. We can tell this because the worker sends back the start time in the response that is being printed by the client.

When work is coalesced, there will be only one instance of that job in the queue at any given time. If a foreground job with a given unique identifier is in the queue and some set of clients request work with the same unique identifier, those clients (along with the first client) are grouped together and are all delivered the same results when the work completes execution. If the requests are for background jobs, then subsequent requests will effectively be ignored if there is still a job in the queue (active or not) with the same unique identifier.

This allows the manager to prevent clients from flooding the queue with the same requests for data. This makes the system more efficient by fanning out the results to multiple clients who are all interested in the same set of results. This also prevents what is sometimes referred to as the thundering herd where an influx of requests or some other event causes a large number of clients request the same work.

Scaling your system

One of the best benefits of building your system to use Gearman is that it provides you with a structured way to scale your system horizontally. This is the ability to solve problems of larger size by adding more nodes to the system rather than simply increasing the processing power of a single node (referred to as vertical scaling.) Even implementing a very basic configuration will provide you with the capability to start small and grow, as you need to.

A very simple Gearman infrastructure would look like the following diagram. Here we have one worker, one client, and one manager:

This setup does not require that you have three physical (or virtual) servers available in order to begin to take advantage of this setup. In fact, you can do it with as little as one server. By starting out this way, you can begin to architect your system to take advantage of this new infrastructure without incurring any additional hardware costs.

However, in practice, it is better to have more managers to rotate through in a round-robin fashion so that your infrastructure looks more like the following diagram:

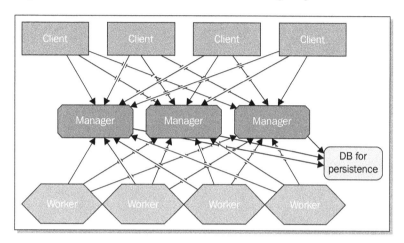

In this scenario the system would be composed of multiple clients, each of whom has a list of managers that it can connect to, and each worker is also connected to (and receiving jobs from) the layer of managers.

By arranging your infrastructure this way, if one of the managers fails, then the workers and the clients still have managers they can interact with, so that work doesn't stop being processed. Your system would be operating at a reduced capacity, but organizing it in this fashion not only provides the system with more capacity but also removes a possible point of failure from the system.

In this example we won't build a system with dozens of managers, workers, and clients; we will build a smaller version by starting two managers as follows:

1. Writing a client that will submit jobs to the two managers.
2. Running the client and watching it submit jobs to both managers.
3. Terminating one of the managers and watching the client submit jobs to the remaining manager.
4. Restarting the manager.
5. Writing a worker to process our jobs.
6. Running the new worker and watching it process jobs from both managers.

Running multiple managers

Open two terminals, and navigate to where you saved the JAR file for the Gearman server. Run an instance of the manager in each terminal, specifying a different listening port on each of them for both the manager and the web interface:

Server 1:

```
java -jar gearman-server-0.6.0.jar --debug \
        --port 4730 --web-port 8080
```

Server 2:

```
java -jar gearman-server-0.6.0.jar --debug \
        --port 4731 --web-port 8081
```

Notice that here we have added the --debug flag on the command line. This is done so that you can see the client's requests being split up between the two servers, and watch all the jobs be submitted to one of them when the other is terminated later on.

Now you have two job managers running on one server. While this obviously won't help alleviate any processing bottlenecks or power-failure issues, it will allow us to demonstrate working with multiple managers.

Writing a client that supports multiple managers

To submit jobs to these managers, we will write a client that will submit jobs indefinitely to two different servers, sleeping for a half a second between requests:

```ruby
#!/bin/env ruby
require 'rubygems'
require 'gearman'


servers = ['localhost:4730', 'localhost:4731']
client = Gearman::Client.new(servers)
taskset = Gearman::TaskSet.new(client)


job_id = 1
while(true)
  data = rand(36**8).to_s(36)
  task = Gearman::BackgroundTask.new("work", data)
  begin
    puts "#{job_id} -- #{data}"
    taskset.add_task(task)
```

```
rescue

  puts 'Problem submitting job'
end
sleep 0.5
job_id += 1
end
```

Submitting jobs to multiple managers

Save this client in a file, `multiserver_client.rb`, and run it to see if it submit jobs to the first server in the list. An example of output from the client might look like the following code:

```
[user@host]% ruby multiserver_client.rb

1 -- squ175ab

2 -- itru5fqp

3 -- jd68o5oz

4 -- vyz49fsc

5 -- v2qrgkzi
```

For each job submitted, the manager will log that it received a SUBMIT_JOB_BG message, and that it responded with a JOB_CREATED message to the client. For every job submitted to the server, you should see something in the server output like the following:

```
19:29:00.403 - [New I/O server worker #1-5] DEBUG org.gearman.server.net.
codec.Decoder - ---> SUBMIT_JOB_BG

19:29:00.403 - [New I/O server worker #1-5] DEBUG org.gearman.server.
net.PacketHandler -   ---> [id: 0x591f9578, /0:0:0:0:0:0:0:1:60072 =>
/0:0:0:0:0:0:0:1:4731] RECEIVED: SUBMIT_JOB_BG

19:29:00.404 - [New I/O server worker #1-5] DEBUG org.gearman.server.net.
codec.Encoder - <--- JOB_CREATED
```

Handling a manager being terminated

When both managers are running, the single client will be submitting jobs to both of the managers, likely in a fairly round-robin fashion. Now, terminate one of the running servers, and verify that the client continues to write its jobs to the other server. You should see twice the level of output from the still-running server.

Now stop the client and restart the recently-terminated manager. Currently the Ruby library doesn't recognize when a manager that it previously had has come back online, but that is outside the scope of this book, so we will simply work around it for now.

Processing jobs from multiple managers

Next, we will write a simple worker that will connect to both servers that we have running:

```ruby
require 'rubygems'
require 'gearman'

# Add two servers to our list
@servers = ['localhost:4730', 'localhost:4731']

puts "Waiting for work from #{@servers.join(', ')}..."
w = Gearman::Worker.new(@servers)
w.add_ability('work') do |data,job|
start_time = Time.now
  puts "#{start_time} Received: #{data}"
  "OK -- #{data}"
end

loop { w.work }
```

Store this in a file, `multiserver_worker.rb`, and run it the same way we have before:

```
[user@host]% ruby multiserver_worker.rb
Waiting for work from localhost:4730, localhost:4731...
```

Notice that the worker is connected to both of our servers and will accept jobs from either of them; you can verify this by watching the logs of both managers. The worker will process all the jobs that are currently in the queue (only the manager that did not terminate will still have jobs).

Now, start the client again and watch as it sends jobs to both managers. Watching the worker output will show that those jobs are processed by the worker. This is a very simple setup but provides you with the basic building blocks to expand out your manager, client, and worker fleet from only a few to hundreds or even thousands.

 Here you can try running multiple clients, workers, and managers and see what happens when you terminate various components in the system.

MapReduce

MapReduce is a technique that is used to take large quantities of data and farm them out for processing. A somewhat trivial example might be like given 1 TB of HTTP log data, count the number of hits that come from a given country, and report those numbers. For example, if you have the log entries:

```
204.12.226.2 - - [09/Jun/2013:09:12:24 -0700] "GET /who-we-are HTTP/1.0"
404 471 "-" "Mozilla/5.0 (compatible; MJ12bot/v1.4.3; http://www.
majestic12.co.uk/bot.php?+)"

174.129.187.73 - - [09/Jun/2013:10:58:22 -0700] "GET /robots.txt
HTTP/1.1" 404 452 "-" "CybEye.com/2.0 (compatible; MSIE 9.0; Windows NT
5.1; Trident/4.0; GTB6.4)"

157.55.35.37 - - [02/Jun/2013:23:31:01 -0700] "GET / HTTP/1.1" 200 483
"-" "Mozilla/5.0 (compatible; bingbot/2.0; +http://www.bing.com/bingbot.
htm)"

206.183.1.74 - - [02/Jun/2013:18:24:35 -0700] "GET / HTTP/1.1" 200 482
"-" "Mozilla/4.0 (compatible; http://search.thunderstone.com/texis/
websearch/about.html)"

1.202.218.21 - - [02/Jun/2013:17:38:20 -0700] "GET /robots.txt HTTP/1.1"
404 471 "-" "Mozilla/5.0 (compatible; JikeSpider; +http://shoulu.jike.
com/spider.html)"
```

Then the answer to the question would be as follows:

```
US: 4
```

```
China: 1
```

Clearly this example dataset does not warrant distributing the data processing among multiple machines, but imagine if instead of five rows of log data we had twenty-five billion rows. If your program took a single computer a half a second to process five records, it would take a little short of eighty years to process twenty-five billion records. To solve for this, we could break up the data into smaller chunks and then process those smaller chunks, rejoining them when we were finished.

To apply this to a slightly larger dataset, imagine you extrapolated these five records to one hundred records and then split those one hundred records into five groups, each containing twenty records. From those five groups we might compute the following results:

Group 1		Group 2		Group 3		Group 4		Group 5	
US	5	Mexico	2	US	15	Italy	1	Finland	5
Greece	4	Scotland	6	China	2	Greece	4	China	5
Ireland	8	Canada	9	Finland	3	Scotland	10	US	10
Canada	3	Ireland	3			US	5		

If we were to combine these data points by using the country name as a key and store them in a map, adding the value to any existing value, we would get the count per country across all one hundred records.

Using Ruby, we can write a simple program to do this, first without using Gearman, and then with it.

To demonstrate this, we will write the following:

✦ A simple library that we can use in our non-distributed program and in our Gearman-enabled programs

✦ An example program that demonstrates using the library

✦ A client that uses the library to split up our data and submit jobs to our manager

✦ A worker that uses the library to process the job requests and return the results

The shared library

First we will develop a library that we can reuse. This will demonstrate that you can reuse existing logic to quickly take advantage of Gearman because it ensures the following things:

✦ The program, client, and worker are much simpler so we can see what's going on in them

✦ The behavior between our program, client, and worker is guaranteed to be consistent

The shared library will have two methods, `map_data` and `reduce_data`. The `map_data` method will be responsible for splitting up the data into chunks to be processed, and the `reduce_data` method will process those chunks of data and return something that can be merged together into an accurate answer. Take the following example, and save it to a file named `functions.rb` for later use:

```ruby
#!/bin/env ruby


# Generate sub-lists of the data
# each sub-list has size = blocksize
def map_data(lines, blocksize)
  blocks = []
  counter = 0
  block = []
  lines.each do |line|
    if (counter >= blocksize)
      blocks << block
      block = []
```

```
      counter = 0
    end


    block << line
    counter += 1
  end
  blocks << block if block.size> 0
  blocks
end


# Extract the number of times we see a unique line
# Result is a hash with key = line, value = count
def reduce_data(lines)
  results = {}
  lines.each do |line|
    results[line] ||= 0
    results[line] += 1
  end
  results
end
```

A simple program

To use this library, we can write a very simple program that demonstrates the functionality:

```
require './functions.rb'


countries = ["china", "us", "greece", "italy"]
lines = []
results = {}


(1..100).each { |i| lines << countries[i % 4] }


blocks = map_data(lines, 20)
blocks.each do |block|
  reduce_data(block).each do |k,v|
    results[k] ||= 0
```

```
    results[k] += v
  end
end
```

```
puts results.inspect
```

Put the contents of this example into a Ruby source file, named `mapreduce.rb` in the same directory as you placed your `functions.rb` file, and execute it with the following:

```
[user@host:$] ruby ./mapreduce.rb
```

This script will generate a list with one hundred elements in it. Since there are four distinct elements, each will appear 25 times as the following output shows:

```
{"us"=>25, "greece"=>25, "italy"=>25, "china"=>25}
```

Following in this vein, we can add in Gearman to extend our example to operate using a client that submits jobs and a single worker that will process the results serially to generate the same results. The reason we wrote these methods in a separate module from the driver application was to make them reusable in this fashion.

The client

The following code for the client in this example will be responsible for the mapping phase, it will split apart the results and submit jobs for the blocks of data it needs processed. In this example worker/client setup, we are using JSON as a simple way to serialize/deserialize data being sent back and forth:

```
require 'rubygems'
require 'gearman'
require 'json'
require './functions.rb'

client = Gearman::Client.new('localhost:4730')
taskset = Gearman::TaskSet.new(client)

countries = ["china", "us", "greece", "italy"]
jobcount = 1
lines = []
results = {}

(1..100).each { |i| lines << countries[i % 4] }

blocks = map_data(lines, 20)
```

```ruby
blocks.each do |block|
  # Generate a task with a unique id
  uniq = rand(36**8).to_s(36)
  task = Gearman::Task.new('count_countries',
                           JSON.dump(block),
                           :uniq =>uniq)

  # When the task is complete, add its results into ours
  task.on_complete do |d|
      # We are passing data back and forth as JSON, so
      # decode it to a hash and then iterate over the
      # k=>v pairs
      JSON.parse(d).each do |k,v|
        results[k] ||= 0
        results[k] += v
      end
  end
  taskset.add_task(task)
  puts "Submitted job #{jobcount}"
  jobcount += 1
end

puts "Submitted all jobs, waiting for results."
start_time = Time.now
taskset.wait(100)
time_diff = (Time.now - start_time).to_i
puts "Took #{time_diff} seconds: #{results.inspect}"
```

This client uses a few new concepts that were not used in the introductory examples, that is, task sets and unique identifiers. In the Ruby client, a task set is a group of tasks that are submitted together and can be waited upon collectively. To generate a task set, you construct it by giving it the client that you want to submit the task set with:

```ruby
taskset = Gearman::TaskSet.new(client)
```

Then you can create and add tasks to the task set:

```ruby
task = Gearman::Task.new('count_countries',
                         JSON.dump(block), :uniq =>uniq)
taskset.add_task(task)
```

Finally, you tell the task set how long you want to wait for the results:

```
taskset.wait(100)
```

This will block the program until the timeout passes, or all the tasks in the task set complete hold true (again, complete does necessarily mean that the worker succeeded at the task, but that it saw it to completion). In this example, it will wait 100 seconds for all the tasks to complete before giving up on them. This doesn't mean that the jobs won't complete if the client disconnects, just that the client won't see the end results (which may or may not be acceptable).

The worker

To complete the distributed MapReduce example, we need to implement the worker that is responsible for performing the actual data processing. The worker will perform the following tasks:

✦ Receive a list of countries serialized as JSON from the manager

✦ Decode that JSON data into a Ruby structure

✦ Perform the reduce operation on the data converting the list of countries into a corresponding hash of counts

✦ Serialize the hash of counts as a JSON string

✦ Return the JSON string to the manager (to be passed on to the client)

```
require 'rubygems'
require 'gearman'
require 'json'
require './functions.rb'

Gearman::Util.logger.level = Logger::DEBUG

@servers = ['localhost:4730']

w = Gearman::Worker.new(@servers)
w.add_ability('count_countries') do |json_data,job|
  puts "Received: #{json_data}"
  data = JSON.parse(json_data)
  result = reduce_data(data)
  puts "Result: #{result.inspect}"
  returndata = JSON.dump(result)
  puts "Returning #{returndata}"
  sleep 4
```

```
  returndata
end


loop { w.work }
```

Notice that we have introduced a slight delay in returning the results by instructing our worker to sleep for four seconds before returning the data. This is here in order to simulate a job that takes a while to process.

To run this example, we will repeat the exercise from the first section. Save the contents of the client to a file called `mapreduce_client.rb`, and then contents of the worker to a file named `mapreduce_worker.rb` in the same directory as the `functions.rb` file. Then, start the worker first by running the following:

```
ruby mapreduce_worker.rb
```

And then start the client by running the following:

```
ruby mapreduce_client.rb
```

When you run these scripts, the worker will be waiting to pick up jobs, and then the client will generate five jobs, each with a block containing a list of countries to be counted, and submit them to the manager. These jobs will be picked up by the worker and then processed, one at a time, until they are all complete. As a result there will be a twenty second difference between when the jobs are submitted and when they are completed.

Parallelizing the pipeline

Implementing the solution this way clearly doesn't gain us much performance from the original example. In fact, it is going to be slower (even ignoring the four second sleep inside each job execution) than the original because there is time involved in serialization and deserialization of the data, transmitting the data between the actors, and transmitting the results between the actors. The goal of this exercise is to demonstrate building a system that can increase the number of workers and parallelize the processing of data, which we will see in the following exercise.

To demonstrate the power of parallel processing, we can now run two copies of the worker. Simply open a new shell and execute the worker via `ruby mapreduce_worker.rb` and this will spin up a second copy of the worker that is ready to process jobs.

Now, run the client a second time and observe the behavior. You will see that the client has completed in twelve seconds instead of twenty. Why not ten? Remember that we submitted five jobs, and each will take four seconds. Five jobs do not get divided evenly between two workers and so one worker will acquire three jobs instead of two, which will take it an additional four seconds to complete:

```
[user@host]% ruby mapreduce_client.rb
Submitted job 1
```

```
Submitted job 2
Submitted job 3
Submitted job 4
Submitted job 5
Submitted all jobs, waiting for results.
Took 12 seconds: {"us"=>25, "greece"=>25, "italy"=>25, "china"=>25}
```

Feel free to experiment with the various parameters of the system such as running more workers, increasing the number of records that are being processed, or adjusting the amount of time that the worker sleeps during a job. While this example does not involve processing enormous quantities of data, hopefully you can see how this can be expanded for future growth.

Scaling this solution

Increasing processing power (vertical scaling) is not the only way to scale a solution. Scaling involves changing the way you think about your data and optimizing your system to take advantage of the resources you have. Building a system that scales means being able to add more capacity as needed in a predictable and manageable way.

One aspect of system optimization is reducing the amount of data that is passed between components of the system. Distributed software can be thought of as one program running on separate systems. In a traditional software program that runs as one process on one system, we look for ways to optimize our program by passing data as references (pointers) instead of passing data as values (copies). In our MapReduce program, we are passing around small amounts of data (a few hundred bytes) between the workers, managers, and clients. Imagine if you tried to take this same approach to processing a multi-terabyte file. It would not make sense to try to transfer hundreds, if not thousands, of megabytes between hosts multiple times.

When working with large objects in your program, you don't want to copy data into and out of functions due to the overhead in CPU time spent copying data as well as the extra memory being consumed by keeping multiple copies of the same data. Because these are distributed pieces of software with no shared memory, and in a lot of cases the data being worked with is so large as to make it impractical to store in memory or send copies around the network, the amount of data being passed between systems should remain as small as possible.

Ideal ways to share data between systems are as follows:

+ Primary keys so the client can retrieve the data itself in an optimal fashion
+ URLs to access the data via an API
+ Paths to shared data storage devices (NFS, SAN, etc.)
+ File offsets (if you are processing the same file from multiple clients)

Additionally, the mechanism for serializing this data is entirely up to you as a developer. Some methods include (but are not limited to) the following:

+ JSON
+ XML
+ BSON (Binary JSON)
+ MessagePack

Processing a large data file

Let's look at how we might use the methodologies we have learned to take advantage of using Gearman to process a logfile that is multiple terabytes in size containing billions of records.

To further build upon our MapReduce program, we could write a client whose job is to look at the size of the file and generate requests to process approximately 50 MB blocks of data, then to take the results and merge them together. To solve such a problem, we would need to take an approach that reduces the amount of data being transferred between the clients, managers, and workers (that is, it does not pass around 50 MB chunks of data). As pointed out before, this data not only has to be transferred from the client to the manager and the manager to the worker (thereby transmitting an amount of data equal to two times the block size), but the manager stores all that data. It is unlikely that the manager would be capable of storing terabytes of job data in memory, and trying to do so would cause the system to fail.

One solution would be to store the data in a location that both clients and workers have access to (network share, or other solution) and then build a client that takes the following approach:

1. The client opens the file to be processed and begins scanning it.
2. For every group of N lines (where N is some number predetermined number):
    ◦ The client determines the beginning and ending byte offset of that set of lines
    ◦ The client submits a background job to the manager for a worker to process with three parameters: path to the file, starting offset, and ending offset
3. Once the file is processed, the client is finished with its work.

This approach ensures that the data being shared between client, manager, and worker is minimal (path, beginning and ending offset) while breaking up the file into blocks of data that can be processed by the worker. Because each block is on the small side, this solution is able to take advantage of having numerous workers on hand, each of which would take the following approach to processing the data file:

1. Receive a job from the manager with the path, starting offset, and ending offset.
2. Open the data file seeking the starting offset.
3. Read a block of data that is (ending offset minus starting offset) bytes in size.

4. Split up the block of data by line-ending.

5. Process each line the same way we processed them in the simple MapReduce example.

6. Submit a job to the manager with the computed data for a different worker to merge with the results from other workers.

Providing job updates

Because we often offload long-running or CPU-intensive work to Gearman (processing a three terabyte logfile in the way we did before might take a very long time), workers and clients are often operating in a disconnected mode. As a result, the worker's status updates are not being delivered directly to the client. To accommodate both the synchronous and asynchronous usecase, Gearman workers can provide periodic data updates, or status updates as they process data.

Here, we will demonstrate these two mechanisms by building the following:

◆ A worker that will periodically send real-time data results to the client

◆ A client that will process real-time data updates

◆ A worker that will emit periodic status updates

◆ A client that will handle status updates

Data updates

In this example, the worker responds periodically with data updates, each one is forwarded to any clients that are listening. These updates are designed to inform clients of the results, not the overall status of the work.

The worker

This is demonstrated in the following example:

```
require 'rubygems'
require 'gearman'

servers = ['localhost:4730']
worker = Gearman::Worker.new(servers)

worker.add_ability('chunked_transfer') do |data, job|
  5.times do |i|
    sleep 2
```

```
    job.send_data("CHUNK #{i}")
  end

  "EOD"
end

loop { worker.work }
```

These periodic updates are emitted as WORK_DATA packets, which when forwarded to the client, should be handled.

The client

In the Ruby client library, an on_data handler is attached to a Task object that processes these data updates. This is shown in the following example:

```
require 'rubygems'
require 'gearman'


servers = ['localhost:4730']


client = Gearman::Client.new(servers)
taskset = Gearman::TaskSet.new(client)


task = Gearman::Task.new('chunked_transfer')
task.on_data {|d| puts d }
task.on_complete {|d| puts d }


taskset.add_task(task)
taskset.wait(100)
```

Status updates

The other way that workers can communicate with a client is to have the worker send periodic status updates. These are different than data updates as they contain an indication of the percentage of work complete, not intermediate results. The status update mechanism operates by having the worker periodically send back a status message containing a numerator and a denominator in order to tell the manager how much of the work has been done. These messages are also stored by the manager internally so they can be used to communicate the progress of both synchronous and asynchronous jobs.

The worker

In this example, the worker uses the `job.report_status` (numerator, denominator) method to inform the manager of its progress. Each time through the work loop, the worker will print a message, sleep for one second and then send a status update to the manager saying that it is one step further in the cycle:

```ruby
require 'rubygems'
require 'gearman'


w = Gearman::Worker.new(['localhost:4730'])


# Add a handler for a "sleep" function that takes a single
# argument: the number of seconds to sleep before reporting
# success.
w.add_ability('sleep') do |data,job|
 puts "Got job with data #{data}"
 seconds = data
 (1..seconds.to_i).each do |i|
   sleep 1
   print i
   # Report our progress to the job server every second.
   # "i" is the numerator, "seconds" is the denominator
   job.report_status(i, seconds)
 end
 puts ". . . Done!"
 # Report success.
 true
end


# Enter our work loop
loop { w.work }
```

The primary difference between the WORK_DATA response and the WORK_STATUS response is that the manager is expected to store the results of the WORK_STATUS message that is sent back by the worker to allow for detached clients to periodically determine the status of their job. The manager stores the numerator and the denominator so that subsequent inquiries by the client using the GET_STATUS message will be responded to with the status of the job in question.

The client

Unfortunately, the Ruby library doesn't have a good way to access a job by the job handle. As a result, this example is written using Python; the following example client will submit a background job that sleeps for six hundred seconds, periodically fetching the job's state:

```python
import json
import time
import gearman
from gearman import GearmanClient


GEARMAN_SERVERS = ["localhost:4731"]


client = GearmanClient(GEARMAN_SERVERS)
jobrequest = client.submit_job("sleep", "600", background=True)


# Get and store the job handle for later lookups
job_handle = str(jobrequest.gearman_job.handle)
completed = 0
total = 0
while((completed == 0) or ((completed / total) < 1.0)):
    # Create the client
    client = GearmanClient(GEARMAN_SERVERS)
    client.establish_connection(client.connection_list[0])
    # Configure the job to request status.
    # The last three arguments are not needed for
    # status requests.
    j = gearman.job.GearmanJob(client.connection_list[0],
    job_handle, None, None, None)
    # create a job request, fake the state
    req = gearman.job.GearmanJobRequest(j)
    req.state = 'CREATED'
    # request the state from gearmand
    response = client.get_job_status(req)
    # the result structure will now be filled
    # with the status information about the task
    completed =  response.status['numerator']
```

```
total = response.status["denominator"]
print "Completed %d of %d" % (completed, total)
time.sleep(5)
```

This Python client will submit a job to the `sleep` queue with the value of `600` as its data, and then, while the job is not 100% complete, it will periodically fetch the status from the manager by sleeping for five seconds between requests, repeating the loop until the job is complete.

Building a processing pipeline

By this point, you should have a pretty good handle on writing Gearman workers and clients. Using these tools, we can build a pipeline of workers for the purpose of data processing with Gearman. In such a system, each worker provides some subset of the overall data processing and passing the completed data to the next system for further processing, storage, and so on. Clients do not have to be their own program; clients are simply any program that submits jobs to a queue. This means that a program could act only as a client and only submit jobs, or it could be responsible for processing jobs as well (that is, both a worker and a client in the system). Building a processing pipeline involves moving work through the pipeline; once a worker is done with processing some data, it will pass the results to other workers.

In the following architecture diagram, a Rails-based web application submits a job to the `resize_image` queue. The image-resizing worker, once it has completed resizing an image, submits jobs to the queues `process_metadata`, `generate_photostream`, and `notify_user` to take further action on the newly-resized image. In this way, the image-resizing worker operates both as a worker and as a client.

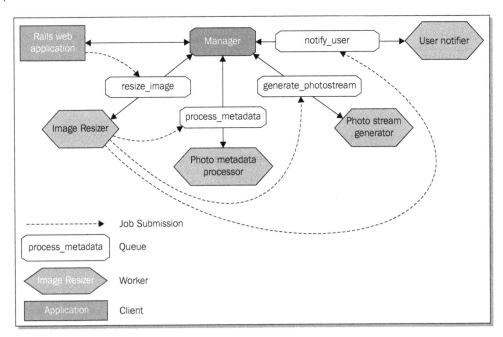

The following example worker demonstrates this type of architecture by resizing an image and submitting jobs to other workers in the pipeline once it is complete to further process the image:

```ruby
#!/bin/env ruby

require 'gearman'
require 'RMagick'
require 'json'

servers = ['localhost:4730',]

client = Gearman::Client.new(servers)
worker = Gearman::Worker.new(servers)
tmpfile = Tempfile.new('image')

worker.add_ability('scale_image') do |jsondata,job|
  data    = JSON.parse(jsondata)
  width   = data['width'].to_f
  height  = data['height'].to_f
  image   = Magick::Image.new (data['full_image_path'])
  format  = data['image_format']
  user_id = data['user_id']

  image.resize!(width, height)
  image.format = format
  image.writetmpfile.path

  job_data = JSON.dump({
        :image_path =>tmpfile.path,
        :user_id =>user_id })
  task = Gearman::BackgroundTask.new("process_metadata", job_data)
  client.do_task(task)
    task = Gearman::BackgroundTask.new("generate_photostream",
  job_data)
  client.do_task(task)
    task = Gearman::BackgroundTask.new("notify_user", job_data)
```

```
  client.do_task(task)
end


loop { worker.work }
```

As you can see in the previous example, once the image is processed, it requests that other workers take on the tasks of processing the image metadata, adding the newly resized image into a live photo stream (possibly a page where all the recently uploaded or resized images are displayed), and then notifies the user that the image was successfully resized.

Using multiple languages

One of the key design goals of Gearman was that it should be language agnostic, allowing for taking advantage of the strengths of various programming languages. Because Gearman is a network protocol, any languages can have first-class support for Gearman. There are libraries for most languages and, if one does not exist, writing a library is a fairly trivial exercise because of the well-documented and straightforward network protocol.

When processing messages, the manager does not inspect anything that is not in the header of the message. The header contains information needed to determine how the manager should handle the message including what type of message is being processed, which queue the message belongs to, the priority of the message, and a few other attributes that vary with the message type.

> To best leverage multiple programming languages, your data will need to be passed between the workers and clients in a format that is not language-specific. All of the examples in this book use JSON as an intermediate format due to the wide array of libraries available for parsing and generating JSON data, but that is not a requirement. Choose whatever serialization mechanism works best for you.

Given this, let's look at some ways that could optimize our example application. Initially, in our example, the web application and workers are written in Ruby. Ruby is not necessarily as well-suited for image processing as others are, giving us a place where we could easily introduce some optimization. Because our architecture is composed of multiple workers using Gearman as the glue between them, we can easily replace various components in the system to take advantage of a worker that is better optimized for a given type of work.

Some enhancements to the system might include:

✦ Replacing our image-resizing worker with one written in C++ using the OpenCV graphics library.

✦ Running that worker on cloud servers with dedicated GPUs to make image processing even faster (OpenCV CUDA functions can operate as much as 20-30 times faster than CPU-based operations on images).

Persistence engines

Gearman managers have two main modes of operation:

+ Non-persistent, in-memory temporal storage
+ Write-through in-memory storage with a persistent storage engine

Depending on your needs and the server you are using, you can adjust this behavior. In the daemon, we are using the persistence engines that are designed to store the actual job data while the data stored in memory is the minimal set of data required to perform jobs. In the case where no persistence engine is chosen, the behavior is to have an in-memory persistence engine. In this mode of operation, any termination of the manager will result in a loss of jobs as they are only stored in memory. Some daemons have modes where they will operate only in-memory but will persist the contents of their memory to disk if they are shutdown cleanly.

Why is this important?

This information is important because there are a few different impacts that this has on both performance and expected behavior. Any time you introduce persistence there will be degradation in performance due to the time required to store the data on-disk, and optionally verify that it was written. This performance hit will vary based on a variety of factors such as the frequency that data is persisted (that is, write-through or write-behind strategies), the storage medium being written to, and network conditions. It is left up to the reader to test out the various implementations being evaluated and determine which, if any, persistence technologies to put in place in their production environment.

Persistent versus non-persistent

The cost of performance is reliability. In-memory queues are the highest performing because they don't have to wait for the data to be stored a second time. However, when using an in-memory-only data store, any number of issues can cause you to lose your job queues such as power failure, system errors, or simply incorrectly terminating the process. It is important to remember that in this mode, if the service terminates, the queues are lost as well.

Depending on your situation, the loss of jobs may have no significant impact on the overall functionality of the system. If, for example, you have a system that uses Gearman to periodically process all the files in a given directory every minute where jobs were routinely being recreated, the memory-only queues would provide the highest throughput. If the manager is terminated and loses the job queues, but is brought back online within a few minutes, then only a few minutes of processing would be lost.

However, in other cases and for a variety of reasons, it is critical that a job that is submitted be completed. Perhaps the data that is being passed to the job is unique and cannot be regenerated (such as a new user sign up) or the process has a very long window between runs (such as a specific job that only runs once per week). In these types of usecases, the manager must guarantee to the client that once the manager has told the client that the job has been created, a worker will process the job at some point.

How safe is safe?

The degree to which that data is guaranteed is up to you—the backing data store could vary between Redis, PostgreSQL, MySQL, Riak, or any number of other storage engines that the servers can talk to. On one end of the spectrum you might use Redis for fast, reasonably-safewrite-behind data storage; on the other you might choose to use a PostgreSQL cluster with guaranteed transactional storage, streaming replication, and hot failover. Each of these configurations comes with its own set of concerns and performance impacts; which one you choose will depend on your environment and your storage needs.

Gearman provides us with a mechanism and the infrastructure required for developing scalable, multiplatform, and parallel systems. By learning to use it in your applications, you can build systems that are capable of easily processing large amounts of data. Additionally, you can use Gearman's asynchronous features to offload data processing from the frontend to backend systems, allowing your user interface to be responsive and flexible. Whether you are moving sign up processing to the background or implementing data crunchers that process gigabytes of geospatial data, having tools like Gearman in your tool belt can help you to solve a number of difficult problems as well as provide you with the tools you need to handle your application's growth.

People and places you should get to know

There are a number of available resources to help you to continue explore using Gearman in your application's infrastructure.

Client libraries

There are a number of libraries for various languages. Here are some of the more popular ones:

- ✦ Node.js: This is a fairly active Node.js Gearman client. More information on this can be found at `https://github.com/mreinstein/node-gearman`.

- ✦ Ruby: Official Ruby library is available as a Ruby gem, maintained by the author of this book. More information on this can be found at `https://github.com/johnewart/gearman-ruby`.

- ✦ Perl: This is the most official Perl library around. More information on this can be found at `http://search.cpan.org/dist/Gearman/`.

- ✦ Python: This is the 2.x branch of the Python Gearman library, maintained by the folks at Yelp. More information on this can be found at `https://github.com/Yelp/python-gearman/`.

- ✦ Java: Information on Java can be found at `https://code.google.com/p/java-gearman-service/`.

- ✦ C#/.NET: One of two C# client libraries are available. This is also developed and maintained by the author of this book. More information on this can be found at `https://github.com/johnewart/gearman.net`.

- ✦ PHP: A library for Gearman in the PECL repository. Go through the links `http://pecl.php.net/package/gearman` and `http://pear.php.net/package/Net_Gearman/` for advanced information.

Another PHP library for Gearman is available in the PEAR repository.

Community

There are a number of community-based resources available on the Internet. The primary method of communication around the Gearman project is the mailing list as well as an IRC channel:

- ✦ Official Google Group: This is a fairly active (1-10 messages per day) mailing list for users and developers of Gearman projects. More information on this can be found at `http://groups.google.com/group/gearman`.

- ✦ IRC chat room: Available on any FreeNode IRC network server as #gearman. More information on this can be found at `irc://irc.freenode.net/#gearman`.

Thank you for buying
Instant Parallel Processing with Gearman

About Packt Publishing

Packt, pronounced 'packed', published its first book "*Mastering phpMyAdmin for Effective MySQL Management*" in April 2004 and subsequently continued to specialize in publishing highly focused books on specific technologies and solutions.

Our books and publications share the experiences of your fellow IT professionals in adapting and customizing today's systems, applications, and frameworks. Our solution based books give you the knowledge and power to customize the software and technologies you're using to get the job done. Packt books are more specific and less general than the IT books you have seen in the past. Our unique business model allows us to bring you more focused information, giving you more of what you need to know, and less of what you don't.

Packt is a modern, yet unique publishing company, which focuses on producing quality, cutting-edge books for communities of developers, administrators, and newbies alike. For more information, please visit our website: www.packtpub.com.

Writing for Packt

We welcome all inquiries from people who are interested in authoring. Book proposals should be sent to author@packtpub.com. If your book idea is still at an early stage and you would like to discuss it first before writing a formal book proposal, contact us; one of our commissioning editors will get in touch with you.

We're not just looking for published authors; if you have strong technical skills but no writing experience, our experienced editors can help you develop a writing career, or simply get some additional reward for your expertise.

Instant Chef Starter

ISBN: 978-1-78216-346-6   Paperback: 70 pages

A practical guide to getting started with Chef, an indispensable tool for provisioning and managing your system's infrastructure

1. Learn something new in an Instant! A short, fast, focused guide delivering immediate results.

2. Learn the core capabilities of Chef and how it integrates with your infrastructure.

3. Set up your own Chef server for managing your infrastructure.

4. Provision new servers with ease and develop your own recipes for use with Chef.

Ruby and MongoDB Web Development Beginner's Guide

ISBN: 978-1-84951-502-3   Paperback: 332 pages

Create dynamic web applications by combining the power of Ruby and MongoDB

1. Step-by-step instructions and practical examples to creating web applications with Ruby and MongoDB.

2. Learn to design the object model in a NoSQL way.

3. Create objects in Ruby and map them to MongoDB.

Please check **www.PacktPub.com** for information on our titles

Clojure Data Analysis Cookbook

ISBN: 978-1-78216-264-3   Paperback: 342 pages

Over 110 recipes to help you dive into the world of practical data analysis using Clojure

1. Get a handle on the torrent of data the modern Internet has created.

2. Recipes for every stage from collection to analysis.

3. A practical approach to analyzing data to help you make informed decisions.

PHP and MongoDB Web Development Beginner's Guide

ISBN: 978-1-84951-362-3   Paperback: 292 pages

Combine the power of PHP and MongoDB to build dynamic web 2.0 applications

1. Learn to build PHP-powered dynamic web applications using MongoDB as the data backend.

2. Handle user sessions, store real-time site analytics, build location-aware web apps, and much more, all using MongoDB and PHP.

3. Full of step-by-step instructions and practical examples, along with challenges to test and improve your knowledge.

www.ingramcontent.com/pod-product-compliance
Lightning Source LLC
Chambersburg PA
CBHW060442060326
40690CB00019B/4299